STEP INTO
SCIENCE

GREEN THUMBS UP!

The Science of Growing Plants

BARBARA TAYLOR

RANDOM HOUSE 🏠 NEW YORK

GROWING PLANTS

In this book, you will discover how to grow plants from cuttings, seeds, and bulbs and how the environment affects plant growth.

The book is divided into six different subjects. Watch for the big headings with a circle at each end—like the one at the top of this page. These headings tell you where a new subject starts.

Pages
4–17

Growing New Plants

Bulbs and tubers; stem and leaf cuttings; sprouting seeds; seed dispersal; spores from mosses, mushrooms, ferns, and lichens.

Pages
18–26

Water, Light, Air, Warmth

Seeds and water; roots and water; water pipes inside plants; cacti; bottle gardens; growing toward the light; water plants; seasons.

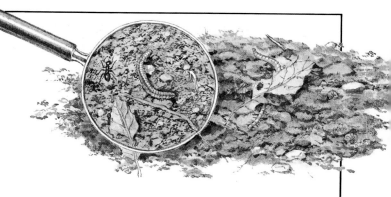
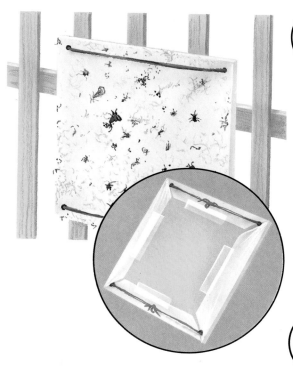

GROWING NEW PLANTS

Have you ever grown a plant from a carrot top? If you put the top of a carrot in a saucer of water, it will sprout leaves. The leaves use the food stored in the carrot to grow. How soon do the leaves appear?

You could also grow plants from the tops of other fruits or vegetables, such as pineapples, parsnips, and turnips. How are they different from the carrot?

Pineapple top

▼ How many different kinds of bulb flowers can you see in this picture? Since each new bulb is exactly the same as its parent, people can grow lots of bulbs which are exactly the same.

Seeds, Bulbs, and Cuttings

There are lots of different ways to grow plants. Here are the three main ways.

We can grow some new plants from seeds which are produced in flowers. Each seed may grow into a new plant that is different from its parent plant.

Seeds

Some plants grow long, spindly stems and sprout new plants at intervals along the stem. These new plants are identical to their parent plants.

Runner

Other new plants grow from pieces of old plants, such as bulbs or cuttings of stems or leaves. These new plants are also identical to their parent plants.

Bulb

Cutting

5

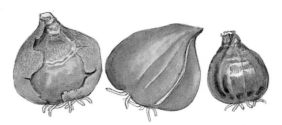

 ## Looking Inside Bulbs

A bulb is an underground stem. It is made up of a flattened stem and a bud surrounded by short swollen leaves. The leaves are full of stored food. In winter, leaves above the ground turn brown and die. Next spring new leaves grow, using the food stored in the bulb.

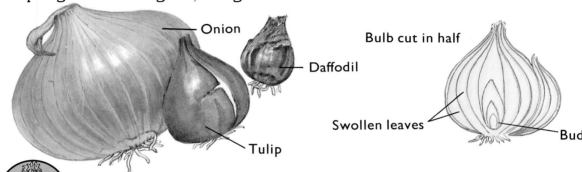

— Onion

— Daffodil

Bulb cut in half

Swollen leaves

Bud

Tulip

Growing Bulbs

Shoot

Bulb

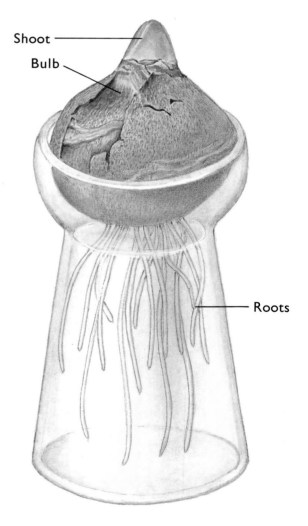

Roots

If you grow a bulb, such as a hyacinth, in water, you will be able to watch the roots develop.

1. Find a jar with a thin neck and fill it with water almost up to the neck. Place the bulb in the neck of the jar.
2. Place the jar in a cool, dark place until you can see a shoot pushing out of the top of the bulb and the roots are about 4 inches long.
3. Move the bulb to a warm, light place to finish growing. Make sure the jar is always full of water. How long does it take for the shoot to appear? How long do the roots grow?

Potting Potatoes

Like bulbs, potatoes are a kind of underground stem. They are called tubers. Tubers store food both to produce new plants and to help the plant survive underground when conditions are not good for growing. The "eyes" of a potato are really buds, which will sprout into shoots and grow leaves. You can grow several new plants from one potato.

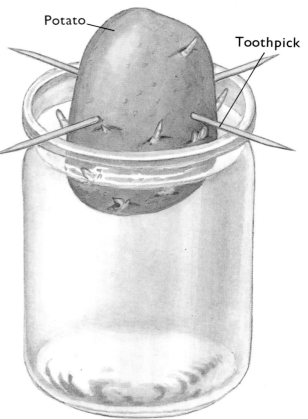

Potato

Toothpick

1. Push four toothpicks into one end of a potato.
2. Balance the potato over a glass jar full of water. Make sure the jar is always kept full.
3. In a few days, shoots will grow from the eyes. Take the potato out of the water and ask an adult to help you cut out each shoot, with a little piece of potato behind it.
4. Plant each shoot in a separate plant pot, covering completely with potting soil.

Growing Bits of Plants

You will need:

lots of containers (such as old yogurt cups, plastic bottles or cups, old egg cartons or food trays), potting soil, thin sticks, a trowel, labels, notebook and pencil, plastic bags, rubber bands, scissors, cuttings from different plants (see below).

Plastic bags

Cup

Yogurt cup

Small stick

Labels

Spoon

Pen

How to Take Stem Cuttings

Cut off the tips of side shoots or young stems without flowers in the summer months. This is when plants do most of their growing. Ask an adult to help you make a clean cut just below a leaf node with a pair of scissors or a sharp knife. Make the cuttings about 3 to 4 inches long and strip off the lower leaves. Stand the cuttings in a container of water until they grow roots, then plant them in soil.

Cactus

Geranium cutting

You can also plant offshoots which sprout from bigger pla

Spider plant

Place each cutting carefully in a hole.

Water the soil well.

Cover each container with a plastic bag.

1. Make some holes in the bottom of your containers and put a few small stones in the bottom. This helps water to drain away so the soil will not get waterlogged.

2. Fill each container with potting soil.

3. Use the stick to make one or more holes in the soil.

4. Place one cutting carefully in each hole, taking care not to bend or crush the cutting.

5. Put a little more soil around the cuttings. Press the soil down firmly so that the cuttings stand upright.

6. Over a sink or outside, fill the container to the brim with water and let the water drain through.

7. Cover each container with a plastic bag and hold the bag in place with a rubber band (see page 20).

8. After a few days, take off the bag. Keep the soil warm and damp.

9. The cuttings should eventually grow more roots and new leaves, but be patient—this won't happen overnight! When some new leaves have grown, transplant each cutting into its own container.

What happens

When you take a cutting from a plant, it can grow new roots and leaves to survive on its own. The parent plant may also sprout new shoots and leaves to replace those you cut off. This is possible because plants (unlike animals) grow all through their lives. Growth is concentrated in certain areas, such as the tips of roots and shoots.

 **More Leaves**

Plants with thick, hairy, or fleshy leaves can be grown from leaf cuttings. The best time to take leaf cuttings is from June to September. You will need the same materials as for stem cuttings (see page 8). Plant several leaf cuttings in a pot of damp potting soil. Cover the pot with a plastic bag to keep the air around the cuttings moist. Look at page 20 to see how this works. When the cuttings have sprouted new leaves, separate them carefully, without breaking the roots if possible. Move each cutting to its own pot and leave it in a warm, shady place for a few weeks until it is growing well. How long do your cuttings take to sprout new leaves?

Jade Plants

Jade plants can be grown from just one leaf. Carefully pull a few leaves off a plant and let them dry. Then plant the leaves so they just stand up in the soil. They should grow new shoots in a couple of weeks.

African Violets

African violets will also grow from leaves. Ask an adult to help you cut a young, healthy leaf off the plant. Make sure it is a clean cut with some leaf stalk attached. When you plant the stalk, keep the leaf itself clear of the soil.

Jade plant

African violet

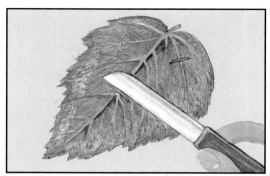

1. Cut main veins under the leaf

2. Weight the leaf down with pebbles

3. New plants sprout from cuts

A New Begonia

With a big enough leaf, you can grow several new plants from one leaf.
Begonias can be grown like this. Choose a large, healthy leaf and cut it
off the plant. Ask an adult to help you make cuts underneath the leaf
on the main veins. Lay the leaf on top of the potting soil with the cut
side down. Weight the leaf with some pebbles to keep it near the soil
and watch what happens.

How many new plants can you grow from one leaf? How long do
they take to grow? Place your cuttings in different places around the
room. Does this make any difference to how they grow?

 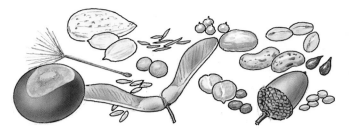

Sorting Seeds

Go on a seed hunt in gardens, hedges, woods, and fields to make your own collection of seeds. You will also find some seeds in wild bird food. Do not forget the seeds we eat, such as rice, corn, oats, nuts, beans, and peas, or the seeds inside fruits, such as peaches or apples. How are your seeds the same? How are they different? See how many ways you can sort your collection into groups. Here are some ideas: size, weight, wild seeds, seeds from trees, or seeds from the farm.

As well as measuring seeds with a ruler, you could also see how many will fit into an egg cup or a square 4 inches by 4 inches.

Small seeds

Can you make a picture with some of the different groups of seeds in your collection? Stick the seeds on to colored cardboard.

Mosses, Ferns, and Lichens

Mosses, ferns, lichens, and fungi do not have flowers, so they cannot make seeds. Instead, they produce spores, which are very small, simple structures. A spore usually consists of one cell and does not have a store of food. If a spore lands in a suitable place, it may grow into a new plant.

Moss spore case on stalks

Fern spore cases under the leaves

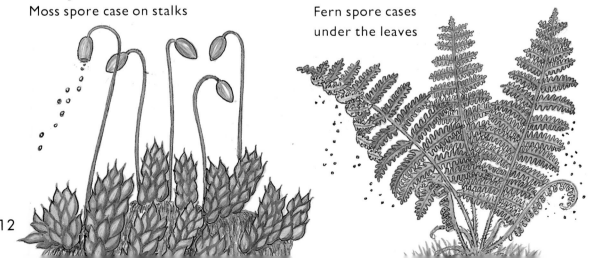

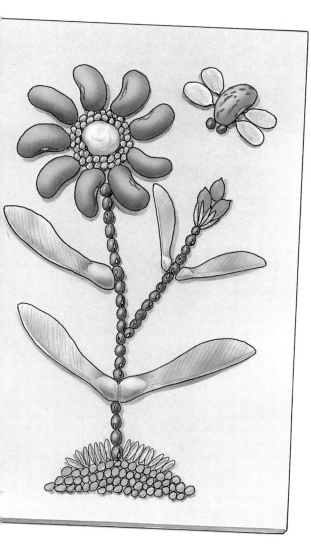

 Mushroom Patterns

The spores of the mushrooms we eat are produced under the cap. To make a spore print, cut off the cap and lay it down on some white paper. Cover the mushroom with a box or a jar to keep out the drafts, and leave it overnight. The pattern you will see the next day is made by the spores that fell off the cap.

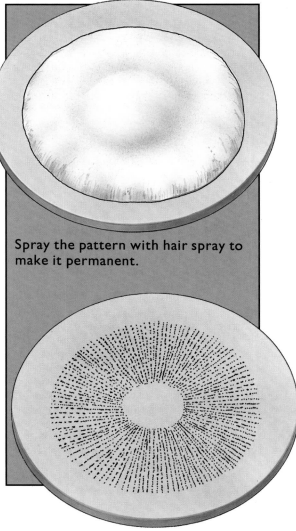

Spray the pattern with hair spray to make it permanent.

◀ Lichen spores may be in disks, cups, or spheres.

Seeds on the Move

Have you ever noticed all the little seedlings growing under a tree? If seeds sprout too close to their parent plant, they will not have enough space, light, or water to grow. They stand a better chance of growing and surviving if they move farther away.

Some plants have special ways of shooting out their seeds so they land some distance away. Squirting cucumber seeds can end up 25 feet away from their parent plant. But most seeds rely on the wind, water, or animals to move them to a new home.

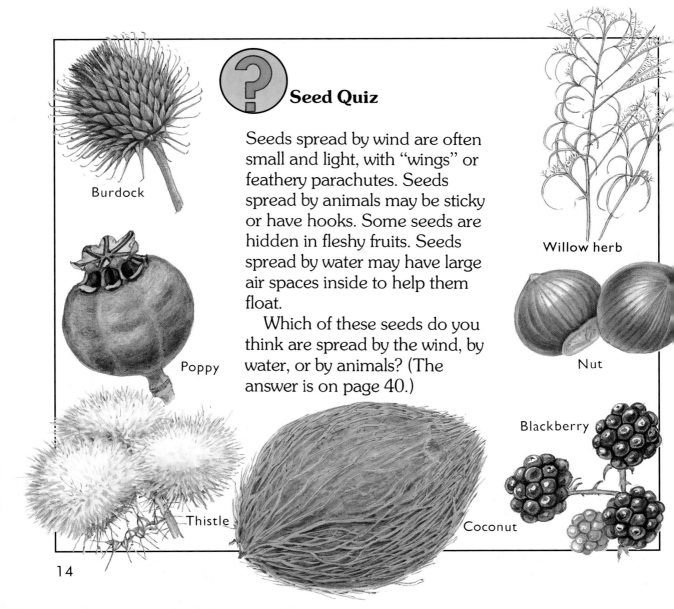

? Seed Quiz

Seeds spread by wind are often small and light, with "wings" or feathery parachutes. Seeds spread by animals may be sticky or have hooks. Some seeds are hidden in fleshy fruits. Seeds spread by water may have large air spaces inside to help them float.

Which of these seeds do you think are spread by the wind, by water, or by animals? (The answer is on page 40.)

Burdock

Poppy

Thistle

Coconut

Willow herb

Nut

Blackberry

▲ Some plants hide their seeds inside tasty berries to encourage animals or birds to eat them. These seeds pass through an animal's insides unharmed and grow into new plants.

 Grow an Avocado Tree

You can grow unusual house plants from avocados or dates.

1. Stick toothpicks into the sides of an avocado pit. This encourages the roots to grow.
2. Balance the pit over a jar of water so that it is just touching the level of the water.
3. When some short roots have grown, take the pit out of the jar and plant it in a container of potting soil (see pages 8 and 9).

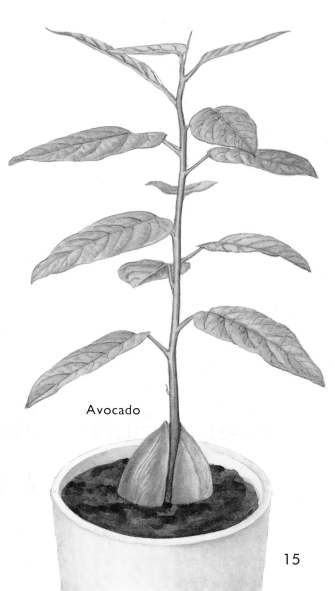

Avocado

Which Way Is Up?

1. Soak some fresh bean seeds in water overnight.
2. With an adult's help, cut a piece of blotting paper to fit around the insides of two large jars with wide necks.
3. Push crumpled paper towels into the middle of the jars.
4. Push a few soaked seeds between the blotting paper and the side of the jar. Place the seeds in different positions—vertical, horizontal, and at an angle.
5. Keep the jars in a warm place out of direct sunlight. Water the paper towels regularly to keep the blotting paper moist.
6. After a few days, roots and shoots will start to appear. This is called germination. Which grows first—the roots or the shoots? In which direction do the roots and shoots grow?
7. When the roots and shoots are a few inches long, turn one of the jars upside down. What happens?

What happens
Roots usually grow down because they are attracted by the pull of the earth's gravity. Gravity is a strong, invisible force that pulls *everything* toward the middle of the earth. The shoots always grow upward toward the light.

Investigating Seeds

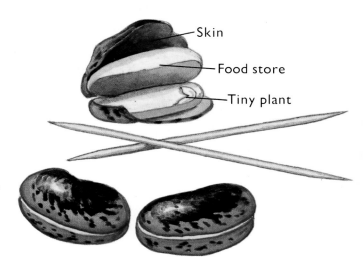

Skin

Food store

Tiny plant

Use toothpicks to take apart some different seeds, such as beans, peas, or wheat. First peel off the seed skin, called the testa. The testa is a tough, waterproof coat that protects the seed. Water gets into the seed through a tiny hole in the testa called the micropyle.

Inside the testa, you should be able to see a tiny plant and one or two seed leaves. A bean has two large seed leaves. Which other seeds have two seed leaves? Can you find any seeds with one seed leaf? Sometimes the seed leaves contain stored food.

Growing Seeds

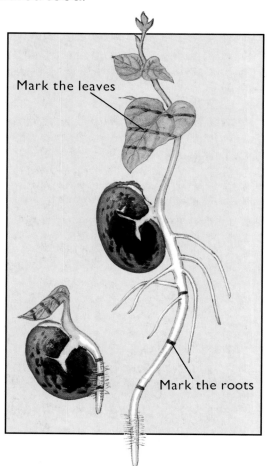

Mark the leaves

Mark the roots

See if you can measure and compare the growth of different seeds. Cress seeds grow quickly, but bean seeds are bigger and easier to measure. Take one of the seeds out every day and measure the roots, shoots, and leaves. Mark the edge of a leaf or the tip of a root so you can see where most of the growing is taking place. Do the plants grow all over or just at the edges?

WATER, LIGHT, AIR, WARMTH

How does the environment around a plant affect the way it grows? Four of the most important factors are water, light, air, and temperature. To investigate water, make four equal groups of cress seeds and soak three overnight.

 Plants and Water

Seeds

Covers

1. In the first container, put some wet seeds on wet cotton balls.
2. In the second container, put wet seeds on dry cotton balls.
3. In the third container, put another group of wet seeds on top of dry cotton balls. Cover the seeds and cotton with water. Keep these seeds and those in the first container damp.
4. In the last container, put the dry seeds on top of dry cotton balls. Cover all containers and leave for a few days.

What happens

Seeds need the right amount of water to germinate properly. Dry seeds on dry cotton will not grow at all. Wet seeds on dry cotton will shrivel up and die. Seeds under water will rot. Only wet seeds on wet cotton grow well.

Make a clown from modeling clay, leaving a dip in its head. Put damp cress seeds on damp cotton balls in the dip. Watch the clown's hair grow.

Roots and Water

1. Place a clay flowerpot full of water in a large bowl.
2. Pack a mixture of soil and sawdust around the pot.
3. Put some soaked peas on the surface of the soil.
4. After a few days, brush the soil off the peas. In which direction are the roots growing?

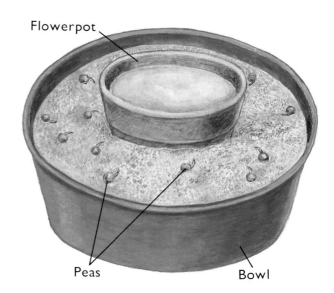

Flowerpot

Peas

Bowl

What happens

When the only source of water is in the flowerpot, the roots grow sideways toward the water. Water is so important to the seeds that the need for water overcomes the pull of gravity.

▼ Rice is planted in fields which are flooded with water. These are called paddy fields. Rice grows well with its roots in lots of water and its shoots in the air.

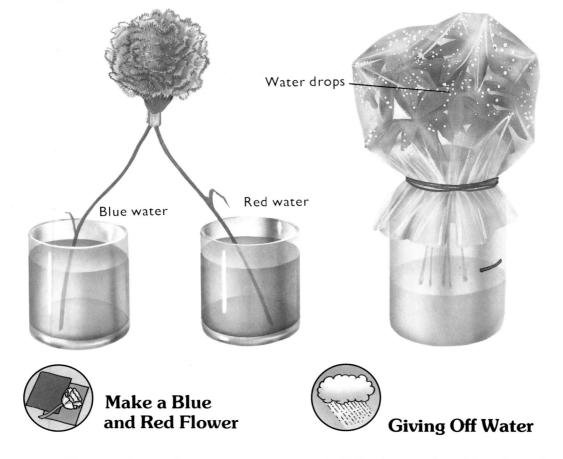

Water drops

Blue water

Red water

Make a Blue and Red Flower

Giving Off Water

1. Fill one of two clean containers with blue food coloring and water.
2. Fill the other container with red food coloring and water.
3. Carefully split the stem of a white carnation from the bottom to the top. Put one half of the stem in the blue water and the other half in the red water.
4. After several hours, some of the petals will turn blue and some will turn red. How long does your flower take to change color?

1. Fill a large plastic bottle with water and mark the water level.
2. Place a plant in the water.
3. Put a plastic bag over the plant and secure the bag to the bottle with a rubber band.
4. Leave the plant in the sun for a few days. What happens to the water level? Can you see droplets of moisture on the bag?

What happens
The carnation "drinks" the colored water through thin pipes in its stem into the petals.

What happens
The plant takes up some of the water through its roots. So the water level in the bottle goes down. This water travels up the pipes in the stem and passes out through tiny holes in the leaves.

▲ Cacti have spines instead of leaves, so they do not give off as much water. Spines also collect morning dew and help to shade the plant from hot sun. Animals find it hard to drink water from a plant with spiny prickles. The stems of many cacti, such as saguaros, can expand like an accordion to store water. Their roots spread out in a wide, shallow network to catch as much water as possible when it does rain.

Make a Bottle Garden

Bottle gardens are simple and fun to make and a very good way to watch plants grow.

You will need:
a large glass or plastic container with a top, gravel, charcoal, potting soil, a funnel, long sticks, a stick with a thread spool fixed to the end, a plastic spoon or fork tied to the end of a stick, a sponge on the end of a stick, small, slow-growing plants such as ferns and mosses.

1. Use the sponge on a stick to clean and dry the container.
2. Put the funnel into the neck of the bottle and pour in a layer of gravel, then some crushed charcoal, and finally dry potting soil.
3. Moisten the soil and pack it down firmly inside the bottle with the thread spool on a stick.
4. Use the fork or spoon on a stick to make some small holes in the potting soil.
5. Use the thin sticks to lower each plant carefully into the holes and to cover the roots with soil.
6. Put the top on the bottle to seal any moisture inside.
7. Stand the bottle in a bright corner out of direct sunlight. After a day or so, can you see drops of moisture forming on the sides of the bottle?
8. After a few months, take the top off the bottle to refresh the air and add a little water if necessary.

If you grow plants in a sealed bottle, they will give off water which will run down the sides of the bottle into the soil. This water can be taken up by the plant again. If the water balance is right, you will not need to water your bottle garden for several months.

 **Follow the Sun**

Did you know that some plants, such as sunflowers, turn to face the sun as it moves across the sky? Plants use the energy in light to make their food. A green pigment called chlorophyll absorbs the sun's energy. Plants are the only living things that can make their own food. All animals have to eat plants—or eat animals that have eaten plants.

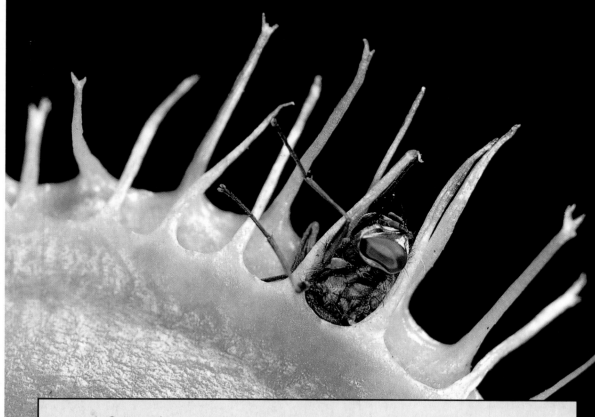

▲ Some plants, such as the Venus flytrap, sometimes trap and eat insects and small animals. They produce digestive juices to break down the meat so they can soak up the nutrients.

Make a Potato Maze

1. Make a small hole in a short side of a long cardboard box.

2. With an adult's help, cut out several pieces of cardboard and stick them inside the box to make a maze like the one in the picture.

3. Put a sprouting potato at the end of the box opposite the hole and place the lid on the box.

4. Leave the box in a light place so that light can easily get into the box through the hole in the end.

5. After a few days, take the lid off the box. Has your potato found the pathway through the "maze" to reach the light?

What happens

The potato senses the light and grows toward it, even though it has to find its way through a maze first. Does your potato shoot eventually grow out of the hole in the side of the box?

Airy Plants

Air bubbles

Air is very important to plants. Can you think why we put water weeds in a fish tank?

Cut a short length of pondweed and leave it in a jar full of water on a sunny windowsill. Look carefully at the leaves. Can you see any bubbles in the water?

When plants make food, they also give off a gas called oxygen. The bubbles given off by the pondweed are bubbles of oxygen. This is the gas that plants and animals, including fishes, need to breathe to stay alive.

 ## Hot and Cold Plants

Keep two similar seedlings at different temperatures to see how this affects their growth. Put one in a warm place and one in a cold place. Make sure both seedlings have the same amount of light so they can make food.

Some seeds, such as apple seeds, need a cold period before they will sprout. In the natural world, this means seeds shed in the fall will not grow until warmer weather returns in spring.

Put apple seeds in the refrigerator for a few days before planting.

In a cool place

In a hot place

SORTING OUT SOILS

Plants need water and minerals from the soil in order to grow well. There are lots of different kinds of soil, such as clay soil, sandy soil, and chalky soil. Some plants only grow well in certain types of soil.

Clay soils hold water and often become waterlogged. In sandy soils, water quickly drains away. In winter, the water in the soil is frozen. Trees with wide, flat leaves cannot draw up enough water to replace that lost from their leaves. So they drop their leaves and rest over the winter.

Collect some soils and see how many differences you can find. What is the texture like? Is the soil smooth, sticky, or gritty? Look at the soil carefully with a magnifying glass.

Separating Soil

Separate the soil by shaking some in a jar of water and letting it soak for a day or two. How many layers can you see? How big are the pieces on the bottom? Are there any pieces floating on the surface? Try this investigation again with different kinds of soil.

Humus

Clay

Silt

Sand

Gravel

Rotten Old Leaves

In the fall, look at the rotting leaves under the trees in a forest, a park, or a garden. This is called leaf litter. Use a magnifying glass to look at the leaves. How are they different from the leaves on a tree? Can you find any leaf skeletons?

When tree leaves fall to the ground, they are gradually broken into pieces as fungi, bacteria, and minibeasts, such as worms, feed on the leaves. The breakdown of leaves, called decomposition, brings the nutrients in the leaves back into the soil to make it rich. Plants can take up the nutrients in the soil and use them to grow.

How Long Do Leaves Take to Rot?

Collect some leaves from different kinds of tree. Bury the leaves under the soil in a container. Label each leaf and keep the soil moist. Every two weeks dig up the leaves to see how much they have rotted away. You may see fungi feeding as a mass of white threads. Then bury the leaves again. Do some leaves decompose faster than others? Some may take years to rot completely and turn into crumbs. But you can watch the start of the rotting process.

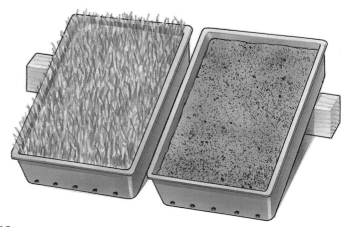

Disappearing Soil

1. Ask an adult to make holes in one end of two seed trays.
2. Fill both trays with soil.
3. Plant grass seeds in one tray. Leave the soil in the other tray bare.
4. When the grass has grown an inch high, prop the trays up on two blocks of wood so they are on a slope. Place a bucket below the holes at the end of each tray.
5. Pour the same amount of water, from the same height, into the end of the trays farthest from the holes. How much soil is washed out of each tray?
6. What happens if you make furrows across the tray with the bare soil and try step 5 again?

▼ Marram grass roots spread in a thick network through the sand. They help to stop sand dunes from being blown away.

Trees grow in two main ways. The twigs and branches grow longer at the tips, so the tree becomes taller and wider. At the same time, the trunk, branches, and twigs grow fatter. Twigs form new buds at the end of the year.

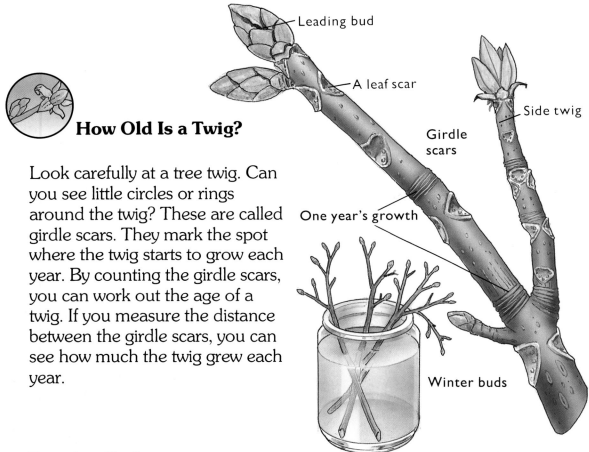

Leading bud

A leaf scar

Side twig

Girdle scars

One year's growth

Winter buds

How Old Is a Twig?

Look carefully at a tree twig. Can you see little circles or rings around the twig? These are called girdle scars. They mark the spot where the twig starts to grow each year. By counting the girdle scars, you can work out the age of a twig. If you measure the distance between the girdle scars, you can see how much the twig grew each year.

Growing Buds

The winter buds on a tree contain the beginnings of the shoot, leaves, and flowers for the following year. The thick, overlapping scales protect the delicate contents of the bud from cold, from insect attack, and from drying out. In spring, bring some twigs indoors and leave them in a jar of water in a warm, sunny place. The best trees to try are horse chestnut, willow, and birch. The buds may take some weeks to open, but you can watch how the leaves unfold and burst out of the scales.

Trees from Twigs

You can grow trees from small pieces of twig. It is better to pull off the twig rather than cut it. Take a small piece of the main twig too. Plant the twig upright in potting soil (pages 8 and 9) or leave it in a jar of water until it has grown some roots, and then plant it. Try this with willow, poplar, or hawthorn twigs.

How Tall Is a Tree?

Here is a simple way to measure how tall a tree has grown. Hold a stick or a pencil in front of you, and walk backward and forward until the top and bottom of the stick or pencil are level with the top and bottom of the tree. Turn the pencil on its side, with the point lined up with the base of the tree. Ask a friend to walk away from the tree at right angles. Stop them when he or she is level with the end of the pencil. Your friend's distance from the tree is the tree's height.

Did You Know?

Did you know that the tallest tree ever was an Australian eucalyptus tree. It measured over 400 feet high—as tall as about 70 people standing on each other's heads!

▲ Bonsai trees start off as normal trees, but they are not allowed to get enough food and water to grow to their normal size. They are miniatures, and their shoots and roots are pruned to stunt their growth. Bonsai trees can take hundreds of years to grow. If you keep trimming the leaves and shoots of a tree seedling, giving it only a little room to grow, you can make your own bonsai tree.